STORYTELLER

Evans Brothers Limited
2a Portman Mansions
Chiltern Street
London W1U 6NR

First published in paperback in 2007

British Library Cataloguing Data
Ganeri, Anita
    Sikh stories. - (Storyteller)
    1.Sikhism - Juvenile literature
    I.Title II.Phillips, Rachel III.Williams,
Rebecca
    294.6

    ISBN 0 237 53235 2
    13-digit ISBN 978 0 237 53235 2

Editor: Victoria Brooker
Series Editor: Su Swallow
Designer: Simon Borrough
Illustrations: Rachael Phillips, Allied Artists
with additional work by Rebecca Wallis
Production: Jenny Mulvanny
Consultant: Rajinder Singh Panesar
text copyright © Anita Ganeri 2001
© Evans Brothers Limited 2001

Printed in China by WKT Co.Ltd

Acknowledgements
The author and publisher would like to
thank the following for permission to
reprint copyright material: page 7 Circa
Photo Library, page 13 Trip/H Rogers, page
16 Trip/H Rogers page 18 Trip/H Rogers,
page 21 Trip/H Rogers, page 25
Trip/H Rogers

VISIT OUR WEBSITE
www.evansbooks.co.uk

STORYTELLER:
SIKH STORIES

Anita Ganeri

Illustrations by Rachael Phillips

Evans Brothers Limited

Introduction

Sikh Stories

 n each of the world's six main religions - Hinduism, Judaism, Buddhism, Christianity, Islam and Sikhism - stories play a very important part. They have been used for many hundreds of years to teach people about their faith in a way which makes difficult messages easier to understand. Many stories tell of times in the lives of religious teachers, leaders, gods and goddesses. Others explain mysterious events such as how the world was created or what happens when you die. Many have a strong moral or lesson to teach.

 he collection of stories in this book comes from the Sikh religion. Sikhs believe in one God who sees and knows everything. He created the world and is everlasting and all-powerful. Sikhs follow the teachings of ten Gurus who taught ordinary people how God wanted them to live. The first Guru was a man called Guru Nanak. He started the Sikh religion in Punjab, in north-west India, at the end of the 15th century. In this book, you can read some of the many stories about the Gurus' lives.

The Ten Sikh Gurus

1 Guru Nanak (1469-1539)

2 Guru Angad Dev (1504-1552)

3 Guru Amar Das (1479-1574)

4 Guru Ram Das (1534-1581)

5 Guru Arjan Dev (1563-1606)

6 Guru Hargobind (1595-1644)

7 Guru Har Rai (1630-1661)

8 Guru Har Krishan (1656-1664)

9 Guru Tegh Bahadur (1621-1675)

10 Guru Gobind Singh (1666-1708)

Contents

The Rich Man and the Needle of Heaven

Guru Nanak was the first Sikh Guru. He spent much of his life travelling around India, teaching people about God. On one of his journeys, he visited the great city of Lahore. A very wealthy banker lived in a magnificent palace in the city. His name was Duni Chand.

When Duni Chand heard that Guru Nanak was in the city, he rushed out to find him. He invited him to a special feast to be held in the Guru's honour.

"Thank you, but no thank you," Guru Nanak said. "I prefer the simple things of life. Besides," he added, mysteriously, "I might cause you some trouble."

But Duni Chand would not take no for an answer. Again and again, he repeated his invitation until Guru Nanak had to accept.

"It will be the finest food you've ever tasted," said boastful Duni Chand.

It was a very splendid occasion. The food was indeed delicious, everyone agreed. When all his guests had finished eating, Duni Chand turned to Guru Nanak.

"I am a very wealthy man," he said. "One of the richest in the whole city. If

there is anything I can do for you, Holy Sir, you only have to ask."

Guru Nanak sat for a moment, deep in thought. He looked around at his luxurious surroundings, the gold and silver, the guests dressed in their finest silk clothes. Then he felt in his pocket and pulled out a small box inside which was a fine, silver needle.

"There is one small thing you can do for me," he told Duni Chand, handing him the needle. "Keep this needle safe and sound, and give it back to me when we meet in the next world."

"Of course, Holy Sir, of course," whined Duni Chand, feeling very important.

When the Guru and his guests had all gone home, Duni Chand rushed to find his wife. He couldn't wait to tell her his good news.

"Guru Nanak must think very highly of me," he said, bursting with pride, "to have trusted me with such a special task. I am to keep this needle and give it back to him in heaven." ▶

Did you know?

Guru Nanak was the first Sikh Guru or teacher and the founder of the Sikh faith. Even as a young child, he was very interested in religion. When he was 30 years old, Nanak vanished for three days. He told people that he had had a vision of God. God had told him to teach people to live in a truthful way and treat everyone as equal. Nanak's followers became known as Sikhs because Sikh means "someone who learns".

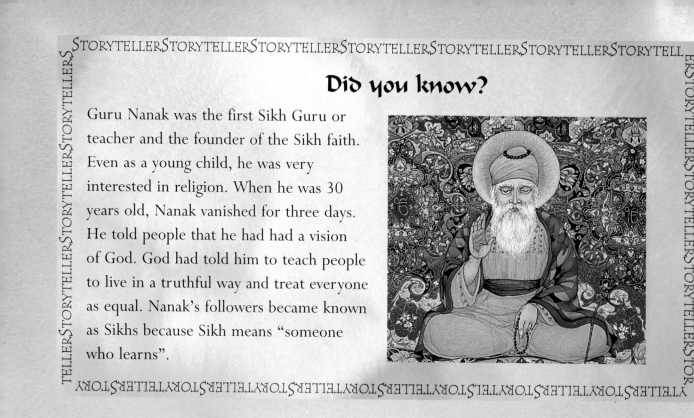

To his astonishment, his wife burst out laughing.

"Oh, my poor husband," she said. "Are you mad? I think you'd better go back and ask the Guru how you are going to do what he wants."

Feeling confused, Duni Chand hurried back to the Guru.

"Oh, Guru Nanak, Holy Sir," he called. "Please tell me how I can take your needle with me when I die?"

Guru Nanak looked at him kindly.

"But the needle is so tiny and light," he said. "If you can't find a way of taking such a small thing with you, what will you do with all your great riches and wealth? How will you take these things with you when you die?"

Duni Chand, the rich banker, felt ashamed as he realised the truth of the Guru's words. All his gold and riches were worth nothing. He couldn't take them with him when he died. From that day on, he

followed the Guru's teachings. He gave his money away to the poor, gave food to the hungry and always tried to help those in need. And when he died, he took many good deeds and good wishes to heaven with him.

Did you know?

The story of Duni Chand shows how being too attached to money or belongings can take you away from the love of God. Guru Nanak teaches Duni Chand that the most important things in life are not gold and riches, but leading a good life and helping other people, whoever they are. That is the way to serve and feel closer to God. Helping others is called sewa, or service. This is a very important idea for Sikhs.

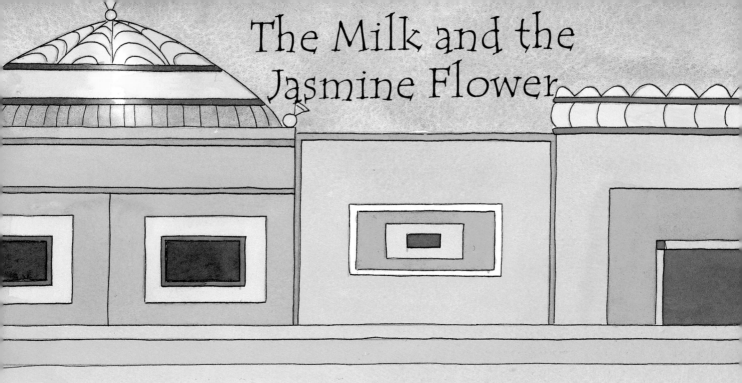

The Milk and the Jasmine Flower

When Guru Nanak went on his travels, he often took Mardana, his faithful companion, with him. Mardana was a musician. One day, after a long and tiring journey, Guru Nanak and Mardana reached the city of Multan. They had been travelling for many days and nights, and Mardana was tired and hungry. He was looking forward to a good meal, and a long, long rest.

Now, at that time, the city of Multan was famous for its many priests and holy men. People came from far and wide to seek their advice, and in return they gave the priests gifts of jewels and money. So the priests and holy men had grown rich and greedy. They didn't want anyone spoiling their good fortune. When they heard that Guru Nanak was nearing their city, they held a meeting to decide what to do.

"We don't want him here," they said. "He'll spoil everything."

So they came up with a plan. They sent a messenger to Guru Nanak, carrying a bowl of milk. The bowl was so full that there wasn't room in it for a single drop more. The message for Guru Nanak was this,

"There are enough priests and holy men here already. There isn't room for any more."

Slowly and carefully, the messenger carried the bowl to where Guru Nanak was staying. Slowly and carefully, in case he spilt a drop, he held the bowl out to Guru Nanak.

"My masters, the priests, have sent you this milk," he said. "Perhaps you have a message for them in return."

Mardana looked longingly at the milk. It looked so cool and refreshing, and he was so thirsty. He hoped that the Guru would ▶

9

take the bowl so that they could both have a drink. But Guru Nanak did not take the bowl. Instead, he picked a sweet-smelling jasmine flower from a nearby bush. He dropped the flower in the bowl. It was so delicate, it floated on the top and not a drop of milk was spilt.

"Here is my message for your masters," Guru Nanak said. "Tell them that there is always room in the world for more goodness and holiness. Just as there is room in this bowl for this tiny flower."

When the priests and holy men heard Guru Nanak's message, they felt ashamed of their rude and selfish behaviour. At once, they apologised to Guru Nanak and gave him and Mardana a very warm welcome to Multan.

Did you know?

Guru Nanak taught that everyone is equal in God's eyes, whoever they are. This is a very important Sikh belief. Guru Nanak taught how important it is to be tolerant and accept other people and their views. Guru Nanak himself was born into a Hindu family but he also had many Muslim friends. In this story, he shows the holy men of Multan that there is room for everyone in the world.

The Story of Bhai Lalo

One day, Guru Nanak and Mardana arrived at a town called Aimanabad. Many of the town's rich and high-ranking people invited Guru Nanak to eat with them, but he always refused. Instead, he and Mardana made their way to the

Did you know?

Every year, in October or November, Sikhs all over the world celebrate Guru Nanak's birthday with a special festival called a gurpurab. The most important part of the festival is a reading of the Sikh holy book, the Guru

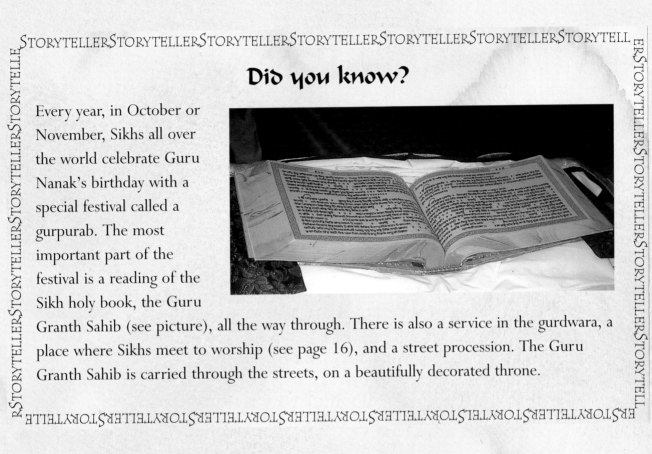

Granth Sahib (see picture), all the way through. There is also a service in the gurdwara, a place where Sikhs meet to worship (see page 16), and a street procession. The Guru Granth Sahib is carried through the streets, on a beautifully decorated throne.

home of a poor but hard-working carpenter called Bhai Lalo. They shared Bhai Lalo's simple food which he cooked himself in his own tiny kitchen.

One day, while they were staying in Aimanabad, Guru Nanak and Mardana received an invitation. It came from a wealthy man called Malik Bhago, a top government official. He was planning a great feast for the most important people in the town, including Guru Nanak. But Guru Nanak refused. Malik Bhago had never felt so insulted in his whole life.

"Why will you not come to my feast" he asked Guru Nanak, angrily, "when you are happy to eat this poor carpenter's food?"

To make Malik Bhago understand, Guru Nanak took two pieces of bread in his hands. One was rough, coarse bread from Bhai Lalo's house. One was fine, seasoned bread from Malik Bhago's kitchen. Guru Nanak squeezed both of his hands. From Bhai Lalo's bread came drops of milk. But from Malik Bhago's bread trickled drops of blood.

"You see, Malik Bhago, why I prefer Bhai Lalo's food to yours," said Guru Nanak. "Your bread tastes good but it is earned by being cruel and greedy. Bhai Lalo's bread may be simple but it is earned by honest and truthful living, and so it tastes as sweet as milk and honey."

Then Malik Bhago understood.

13

The Emperor and the Langar

Did you know?

The word langar means "the Guru's kitchen". It is the meal which Sikhs eat after attending a service in a gurdwara (see page 16). It is also the name of the kitchen in which the meal is prepared. All the members of the gurdwara take turns to prepare and serve the langar, and anyone is welcome to share it, including people who are not Sikhs. Langar is an important way of expressing the Sikh belief that everyone is equal in God's eyes.

Guru Amar Das was the third Sikh Guru. He lived in the village of Goindwal on the banks of the River Beas. Here Guru Amar Das spent his days preaching and in prayer and meditation. He also set up a langar, or kitchen, where everyone could sit and eat together, men and women, rich and poor, to show that all were equal in God's eyes.

One day, the Emperor of India, the great Akbar himself, decided to pay the Guru a visit. Now Akbar was a Muslim but he was also a wise and just ruler who treated all religions with respect. He was eager to visit Guru Amar Das and learn more about the Sikhs. He sent a message to the Guru to tell him that he was on his way. The news sent a stir through the village. The emperor was coming! However would they welcome such an important visitor? Everyone had a different idea.

Guru Amar Das listened to what they had to say and thought about it carefully. Then he told the people,

"There will be no special welcome for Emperor Akbar. Even though he is the emperor, he is also a human being like everyone else and all human beings are equal in God's eyes. Anyone, no matter who they are, should be welcomed with the same kindness and hospitality, be they emperors or beggars."

So this is what happened. When Akbar arrived in the village, he was not met by a welcoming party nor taken to the Guru's house. Instead, he was taken to the langar and asked to sit on the floor with the other guests. Akbar was happy to do as he was asked. He took his place on the floor and shared the same food as everyone else.

The meal that day was very plain and simple, just some bread, rice and lentils. But, to the emperor, it tasted like a feast. He enjoyed every mouthful. ▶

Did you know?

A gurdwara is a place where Sikhs meet to worship. The word gurdwara means "the house of the Guru". It does not have to be a special building. Any place that has a copy of the Guru Granth Sahib can be a gurdwara. Inside there is a room for worship. Here people say prayers, sing hymns and listen to readings from the holy book. When they enter, they remove their shoes and cover their heads. Then they bow in front of the Guru Granth Sahib to show their respect.

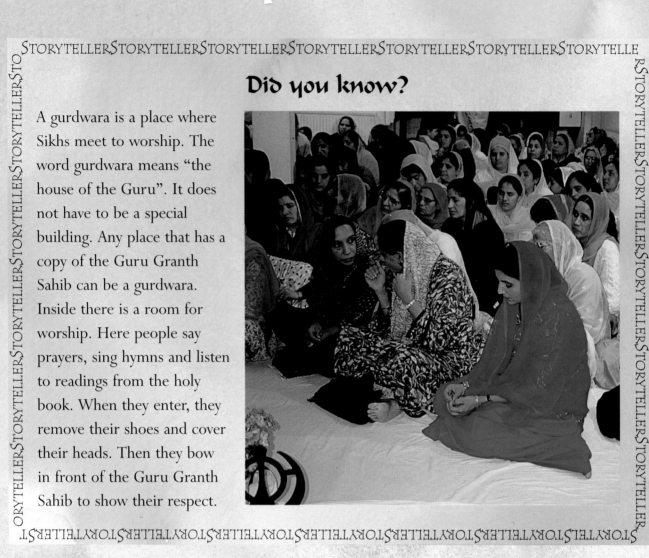

When the meal was over, Akbar went to speak to Guru Amar Das.

"You have so many people coming here to eat," he said. "It must be a hard job to provide so much food. I would be happy to help you. I will gladly give you some good, fertile land on which to grow your crops for langar. Please accept this gift from me."

Politely but firmly, the Guru replied, "You are a good, kind man, Your Majesty. Your intentions are of the very best. But I cannot accept your offer. God provides us with plenty for the langar. Each person in our community gives whatever is needed, as much or as little as they can spare. That is their duty and responsibility. In this way, we all play our part and take our share."

The emperor was greatly impressed by the Guru's words. But still he wanted to help. So he gave a grant of some land to the Guru's daughter for her to put to good use instead. Then he went away from Goindwal, filled with respect for the Guru's teachings.

The Story of Guru Ram Das

There was once a man who lived in Lahore whose name was Jetha, which means "first born". One day, he joined a group of people travelling to Goindwal to visit Guru Amar Das. Jetha was so impressed by the Guru's teachings that he stayed behind to serve him. He was famous for his great humility and did not change a bit, even when he married the Guru's daughter.

One day, Guru Amar Das decided to build a well with steps leading down to it so that people could easily reach the water. Jetha volunteered to help with the work. Some people laughed at him. It was not fitting for the Guru's son-in-law to work as a common labourer, they said. But Jetha took no notice of them.

Now Guru Amar Das was a very old man and the time came to choose his successor. But which of his two sons-in-law should he choose to become Guru after him? He decided to set them a test.

"I want each of you to build a platform" he told them, "according to my instructions."

The two men set to work. When they had finished, the Guru inspected the platforms very carefully.

"These are no good," the Guru said. "Knock them down and start again."

The two men began again. But still their efforts did not please the Guru.

"Take them down and start again," he said. ▶

Did you know?

Guru Ram Das decided that the Sikhs should have a city which would become the centre of their religion. This city became known as Amritsar, in Punjab, northern India. When Guru Ram Das died, his son, Guru Arjan, carried on the building of Amritsar. He built a beautiful gurdwara in the middle of the lake. This is called the Harimandir or "Golden Temple". It is the Sikhs' most important building.

The fourth time this happened, the elder son-in-law decided enough was enough. Jetha, however, carried on. He built a fourth, a fifth, a sixth and a seventh platform before the Guru declared himself happy with his work.

"I choose Jetha to be Guru after me," he told the people who had gathered to watch, "because he has worked very hard and shown great patience and devotion."

So Jetha was given the name Ram Das, or "God's servant". And, when Guru Amar Das died, he became the fourth Sikh Guru.

The Princes and the Guru's Cloak

Once, on a hunting trip deep in the forest, the sixth Sikh Guru, Guru Hargobind, saved Emperor Jahangir's life when a tiger leapt out to attack him. After this, Guru Hargobind and Emperor Jahangir became good friends. But not everyone at the royal court was happy with their friendship. One of the court officials, called Chandu, plotted to get rid of the Guru.

One day, Jahangir became very ill. He grew weaker and weaker, until his doctors feared for his life. In despair, the emperor summoned Chandu.

"Send for the court astrologers," he said. "I will ask them what to do."

Chandu did as he was asked. But before the astrologers were allowed in to see the emperor, he took them to one side.

"Do exactly as I say," he told them, "and I will make you rich."

The greedy astrologers agreed to do as Chandu asked. They told the emperor that he would only get better if he asked a holy man to go to the fort at Gwalior to pray for his recovery.

"But who shall I send?" asked the emperor.

"What about Guru Hargobind?" said Chandu. "No one is holier than he."

So the emperor sent Guru Hargobind to the fort at Gwalior to pray for his good health. Chandu thought he had got rid of him once and for all.

When Guru Hargobind arrived at Gwalior, he found that he was not alone. Fifty-two Hindu princes were also being kept prisoner there. The Guru was treated very well and spent his days in prayer and meditation. But the princes were dressed in dirty rags, and never had enough to eat. Guru Hargobind felt sorry for them and did what he could to help them out. He shared his food and got them proper clothes, and tried to keep their spirits up.

Two years passed. Finally, a message came from the court. The emperor had fully recovered from his illness and Guru Hargobind was free to go. Chandu's plan to keep him out of the way had well and truly backfired. But the Guru refused to leave the fort.

"Your Majesty," he told the emperor, "I cannot leave on my own. Please also release the other prisoners."

The emperor was flabbergasted. He couldn't possibly release all fifty-two prisoners. That would be unthinkable. So he wrote a note to Guru Hargobind,

"My friend, if you can assure me of their good behaviour, some of the prisoners may go free. But only as many as can hold on to your cloak when you leave the fort." ▶

Now the gate of the fortress was very narrow and the emperor had been very clever. Jahangir thought that the Guru would be able to take four or five princes with him, no more. Guru Hargobind thought quickly. He had a special cloak made for him, with fifty-two silk tassels. When the gates opened, it was not four or five, but all fifty-two princes who walked out behind him, each holding on to one of the tassels. The Guru's cloak had saved them all.

Did you know?

Every year, in October or November,
Sikhs celebrate the festival of Divali.
They remember the time when Guru
Hargobind arrived safely back in
Amritsar after his release from prison.
Divali is the festival of lights. People
were so happy to see him that they lit
lamps in their houses to welcome him
home. Today, Sikhs celebrate with
bonfires and fireworks. In Amritsar, the
whole of the Golden Temple is lit up.

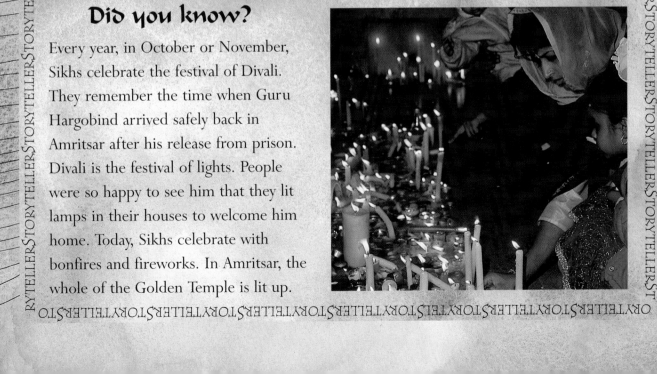

The Merchant and the Five Hundred Gold Coins

Just before he died, the eighth Sikh Guru, Guru Har Krishan, said to the Sikhs who were gathered around his bedside,

"You will find my successor in Bakala," he said. "That is where the next Guru will come from."

Now Bakala was a small village in north-west India. It was usually a quiet, sleepy place but the Guru's dying words caused chaos. Suddenly, the village was filled with people, all claiming to be the next Guru. Many of these were greedy people who accepted money and offerings from wealthy devotees, when they had no right to do so. The confusion lasted for almost a year, without the true Guru being found. Then a strange and curious thing happened...

A wealthy Sikh merchant called Makhan Shah was sailing along the west coast of India. His ship was laden down with fine perfumes and costly silks which he would be able to sell for a fortune. Suddenly, a terrible storm blew up. The wind howled and the rain lashed down. Huge waves tossed the ship from side to side. Makhan Shah had never seen anything like it in all his years of sailing. He knew that his ship could not last for much longer. Sooner or later, it would be smashed to pieces on the rocks. In despair, Makhan Shah closed his eyes and began to pray,

"Dear God, if you will save my ship, I will give the Guru a gift of five hundred gold coins for the good of Sikhs everywhere. If only you will save us."

Makhan Shah's prayers were answered. When he opened his eyes, a strong wind had blown his ship away from the rocks and was guiding it safely towards the shore. He and his crew and his cargo were saved.

When he reached dry land, Makhan Shah remembered the promise he had made. He set off at once to make the long journey to the village of Bakala to give his gift of gold coins to the Guru. But, in Bakala, he faced a dilemma. There were an astonishing twenty-two people, all claiming to be the Guru. Which of them was telling the truth? Who should he give the gold coins to? Who was the rightful Guru? This is what Makhan Shah decided to do.

"I will visit each of these gurus in turn," he thought, "and offer each one just two gold coins. The false gurus will take the money, no questions asked. Only the true Guru will know how much I really promised to give."

So Makhan Shah went from house to house, visiting each of the gurus in turn. In the first house, a man sat cross-legged on a grand chair like a throne. Makhan Shah gave him two gold coins. ▶

"Bless you, my son," said the man, greedily. "How clever you have been to find the one true Guru. Now, what else do you have to give me? That jacket you're wearing looks very fine."

Makhan Shah left the house quickly. This certainly wasn't the true Guru. He was much too greedy and money-grabbing. Makhan Shah went from house to house but all of the gurus he visited turned out to be false. Would he ever find the true Guru? Just as he was beginning to give up hope, he asked an old man if there was anyone else he could think of who might be the Guru.

"Well," said the old man, "there is

someone. He's a holy man called Tegh Bahadur. He lives quietly at the edge of the village, minding his own business. Perhaps he is the person you are looking for. Though he has never claimed to be the Guru."

Did you know?

In 1675, Guru Tegh Bahadur was killed by Emperor Aurangzeb because he refused to give up his beliefs or change his religion. Guru Tegh Bahadur believed that everyone should be free to worship God in the way they thought was right. But Aurangzeb wanted everyone to become a Muslim. He killed many Hindus who refused. The Hindus asked the Guru for help. But the emperor arrested the Guru and cut off his head. Sikhs remember Guru Tegh Bahadur's death every year, in November or December, with a gurpurab festival. In Delhi, a gurdwara was built at a place where the Guru was killed.

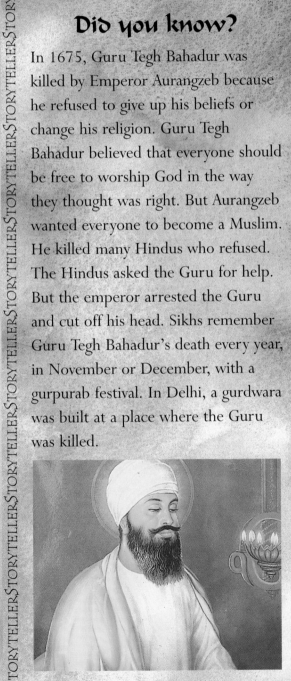

Makhan Shah thanked the old man and hurried off to find Tegh Bahadur. He found him in a small hut at the edge of the village, deep in meditation. Makhan Shah placed the two gold coins in his hand. Slowly, Tegh Bahadur opened his eyes. He looked at the coins, then at Makhan Shah.

"What is this?" he asked. "When your ship was sinking, you promised five hundred gold coins. Why are there only two?"

Makhan Shah was overjoyed.

"At last," he cried, "I have found the true Guru."

He placed the five hundred gold coins in front of the Guru, then ran outside and climbed on top of a roof.

"I have found the Guru!" he shouted at the top of his voice. "I have found the true Guru!"

That night there was great rejoicing in Bakala. For Guru Har Krishan's words had come true. And this is how the ninth Sikh Guru, Guru Tegh Bahadur, was found by a merchant.

Did you know?

This story shows how important it is to have faith in God. Sikhs believe that if you have faith in God, God will find a way to help you to find out the truth. Makhan Shah's faith was rewarded when God helped him to find the true Guru from among all the false and greedy ones.

The Founding of the Khalsa

The tenth Sikh Guru was called Guru Gobind Singh, the son of Guru Tegh Bahadur. This is the story of how he created a close-knit band of good and pure Sikhs, which was called the Khalsa.

One spring day, in the year 1699, Guru Gobind Singh summoned the Sikhs from all over India to come to the town of Anandpur. As was their custom, a huge crowd of Sikhs came from far and wide to celebrate the festival of Baisakhi. But this year there was a buzz of excitement in the air and the feeling that something extra special was about to happen.

When all the Sikhs were gathered together, Guru Gobind Singh stood before them, dressed in his uniform and with his sword in his hand. For many years, the Sikhs had fought hard to defend their faith against their enemies. Now Guru Gobind Singh wanted them to be brave and ready, if need be, to give up their lives for their beliefs.

"It is time for us to be strong," he told them, brandishing his sword. "Now who will give up his life for the Guru and for God? Who is ready to die for his faith?"

The huge crowd fell silent. No one moved, or spoke. The Guru's words frightened them. Whatever should they do?

Again, the Guru repeated his question. "Who is ready to die for his faith?" he said. "Who will offer his head?"

Still nobody replied. A third time, the Guru asked his question. This time a man stepped forward. His name was Darya Ram. He made his way through the crowd to the Guru.

"I will give up my life for the Guru and for God," he said, bravely. "You can take my head."

Guru Gobind Singh led Darya Ram into his tent. A few minutes later, there was a loud thud and the Guru came out, his sword stained with blood. The crowd gasped in horror. Some people began to leave. Others wanted to know what would happen next.

Again, the Guru called out, "Who is ready to die for his faith?"

Another man stepped out of the crowd and was led into the Guru's tent. Once again, when the Guru came out, his sword was stained with blood. Three times more, the Guru asked his question and three more brave men came forward, until five volunteers had been led into the Guru's tent.

Then an extraordinary thing happened. Before the crowd's astonished eyes, the Guru led all five men out of tent, unharmed and alive. They were wearing splendid new saffron robes, with blue sashes and saffron turbans. Each carried a gleaming sword.

"These men have proved their bravery," the Guru told the crowd. "They were ready to die for their faith. From now on, they will be known as the Panj Pyare - the Five Beloved Ones. They are the first members of the Khalsa, the pure ones, chosen by God. Those who wish to join the Khalsa must be pure of heart, brave of spirit and strong in their beliefs. But all may join, men and women, high born and low."

Then the Guru prepared a welcome ceremony for the Panj Pyare. First they drank sweet amrit, the water of life, from the same steel bowl. This showed that they were all equal. Then the Guru himself knelt down and drank amrit.

"I am just the same as you," he said. "The Khalsa is the Guru and the Guru is the Khalsa."

Did you know?

The festival of Baisakhi takes place in April. This is the start of the Sikh New Year. It is also the time when many young Sikhs join the Khalsa. A special ceremony is held in the gurdwara. It is led by five people who stand for the Panj Pyare. There are prayers and readings from the Guru Granth Sahib. The people joining kneel and drink amrit, just as the first Khalsa members did. More amrit is sprinkled on their hair, eyes and hands. By taking amrit, Sikhs accept the rules which the Guru wanted them to follow - accepting all people as equal, helping those who suffer injustice, serving others selflessly and dedicating their lives to God.

Did you know?

When Guru Gobind Singh died, he did not choose a human Guru to come after him. He said that the Guru Granth Sahib should be his successor. From that time on, the Guru Granth Sahib has been the Sikhs' holy book. It is a collection of hymns written by the Gurus and by some Hindu and Muslim holy men. The Guru Granth Sahib is used in all Sikh worship and is treated with great care and respect because it is believed to be the voice of God.

Glossary

Akbar A great emperor of India who ruled from 1556-1605. Akbar was a Muslim but he was interested in all religions.

Amrit A special mixture of sugar and water that is used at Sikh ceremonies.

Amritsar A city in north-west India that is special for the Sikhs. It was founded by Guru Ram Das. Its most important building is the Harimandir.

Astrologers People who tell the future from the position of the stars and planets.

Aurangzeb The last great emperor of India who ruled from 1658-1707. He was a very strict Muslim.

Baisakhi A festival when Sikhs celebrate the start of the New Year and the founding of the Khalsa. It is also the time when many young Sikhs join the Khalsa. It falls in April.

Divali A festival when Sikhs remember the release of Guru Hargobind from prison. It is celebrated in October or November.

Gurdwara A place where Sikhs meet to worship. A gurdwara is any place that contains a copy of the Guru Granth Sahib.

Gurpurab A festival when Sikhs remember the birth or death of one of the Gurus. There is a non-stop reading of the Guru Granth Sahib and a street procession.

Guru Granth Sahib The Sikhs' holy book. It is a collection of hymns and writings by the Gurus and other holy men.

Guru Nanak The first Sikh Guru and the founder of the Sikh religion at the end of the 15th century.

Gurus The ten great teachers of Sikhism from 1499-1708 who taught people how God wanted them to live.

Harimandir A very important gurdwara for Sikhs in Amritsar. It is also called the Golden Temple.

Hindu Someone who follows the Hindu religion which began in India about 4,000 years ago.

Jahangir The Muslim emperor who ruled India from 1605-1627.

Khalsa The name given to the group of Sikhs who have become full members of their faith. The word Khalsa means 'the pure ones'.

Langar A meal eaten by Sikhs after a service in the gurdwara. It is also the kitchen in which the meal is prepared.

Mardana A Muslim musician who accompanied Guru Nanak on his travels.

Muslim Someone who follows the religion of Islam which began in the Arabia about 1,400 years ago.

Panj Pyare The first five members of the Khalsa. Panj Pyare means 'the Five Beloved Ones'.

Punjab A region in north-west India where Sikhism began.

Saffron An orange-yellow colour

Sewa Sewa means 'service', for example, helping other people without any thought of reward.

Sikhism The religion of the Sikhs. They follow the teachings of the ten Gurus.

Sikhs People who follow the Sikh religion. The word Sikh means 'someone how learns'.

Index